Rip Current Rescue

by Monty Ward
illustrated by Tony Sansevero

Editorial Offices: Glenview, Illinois • Parsippany, New Jersey • New York, New York
Sales Offices: Needham, Massachusetts • Duluth, Georgia • Glenview, Illinois
Coppell, Texas • Ontario, California • Mesa, Arizona

Every effort has been made to secure permission and provide appropriate credit for photographic material. The publisher deeply regrets any omission and pledges to correct errors called to its attention in subsequent editions.

Unless otherwise acknowledged, all photographs are the property of Scott Foresman, a division of Pearson Education.

Illustration by Tony Sansevero

Photograph 24 ©DK Images

ISBN: 0-328-13628-X

Copyright © Pearson Education, Inc.

All Rights Reserved. Printed in the United States of America. This publication is protected by Copyright, and permission should be obtained from the publisher prior to any prohibited reproduction, storage in a retrieval system, or transmission in any form by any means, electronic, mechanical, photocopying, recording, or likewise. For information regarding permission(s), write to: Permissions Department, Scott Foresman, 1900 East Lake Avenue, Glenview, Illinois 60025.

7 8 9 10 V0G1 14 13 12 11 10 09 08

From his shoulder blades to his feet, Ben Chavez was a rack of bones and sharp angles. He was skinnier than any other eleven-year-old around. How, everyone wondered, could he swim so long in the ocean without turning blue from the cold?

In fact, his lips did turn a little blue. Goose bumps covered his body. He shivered quite a bit. But none of that was enough to make Ben Chavez want to get out of the water—ever. Each summer when his family visited the beach for two weeks of vacation, Ben spent every moment he could in the ocean. He didn't care if it was windy or cold. The ocean was where he wanted to be.

   Ben loved the feeling of floating. It was a way to beat gravity. Lying flat on his back, with his arms and legs out, he felt as if he were gliding above Earth. When he relaxed and let his limbs hang loose, he imagined that he was a jellyfish. Ben was cushioned by the water on all sides and pulled by the tide.
   Sometimes, Ben opened his eyes underwater. It took a few seconds to get used to it, but what he saw was always worth the salty sting. Everything underwater looked slippery and moved in a sleepy way. If he scooped a handful of sand and let it dribble out, the grains fell back to the ocean floor in slow motion. Looking ahead, as far as he could, the water became a wall of green. It was dark and hazy. The dark green veil was always ahead of him—a trick of light and water.

Ben was a good swimmer, though he had never taken lessons. He could tread water well, and he was able to scoot across the surface quickly and efficiently in his own way.

He also had confidence. Rough water didn't scare him. He liked windy days best when waves churned the ocean. It was thrilling to play in the white froth the waves left behind. Ben liked to feel the pull as the water rushed back toward the sea. He was like a fish, his parents said, and they trusted him in the water.

So no one really noticed one blustery day, when the water was extra choppy, that Ben seemed to be drifting farther from the shore. His parents were distracted by his baby sister and took their eyes off Ben for only a few moments. The family had picked a spot for their picnic far down the beach. It was farther than they had ever gone before. They had wanted to get away from the crowds near the parking lot.

There was something strange about the water on this part of the beach, something that Ben had never noticed in other places. It scared him. He was sloshing near the shore and diving under the waves when suddenly, the sandy bottom disappeared beneath his feet. In that instant the water went over his head. Normally, that would have been just fine. But this wasn't normal. A strong current that seemed to have come from nowhere had grabbed Ben and was shooting him out to sea.

In just seconds the beach, which had been so close, was one hundred feet away. Then it was one hundred twenty feet, and then one hundred fifty feet away! Ben began to swim against the current. The stream of water kept pulling him back. He kicked and pulled harder in a frantic attempt to get to shore, but still he made no progress.

Stunned, Ben tried shouting, but no one heard him over the wind and the waves. He waved one arm, hoping someone on the beach would see him. He couldn't tell if anyone saw him. His legs and arms ached. How much longer could he stay afloat? The choppy sea slapped at his face, forcing salty water up his nose.

The last thing Ben remembered was trying to open his mouth for a gulp of air just as a powerful wave smacked against his head. Ocean water rushed into his mouth, clogged his throat, and blocked his breathing. He gasped. More water gushed in, stealing his last bit of air.

When Ben woke up, he was lying flat on his back on the beach. He opened his eyes and blinked. A strange man was bent over him. Ben's mother and father were kneeling on either side of him.

"Are you all right?" asked the man.

Ben nodded slowly. He was too tired to speak. What had happened?

"This is a rough part of the beach," Ben heard the man tell his parents. "The rip current will take you right out. Luckily I got to him before he went under."

The man turned and smiled at Ben.

"You're a fighter," he said. "I can tell you're a good swimmer. Next time, don't panic. Ride the current out and you'll be OK."

Ben lay there, glad to feel the firm sand beneath his back. He knew he wouldn't forget that advice. He would learn everything he could about rip currents. Ignorance had gotten him into trouble. He never wanted to be trapped like that again.

* * * * *

Now, as a young man of nineteen, Ben had tried to explain the danger of rip currents to swimmers at Wayside Beach many times. Ben sometimes wondered if his message ever got across to the swimmers.

This was his second summer working as a lifeguard at Wayside. It was almost the perfect job. He could swim in the ocean every day. With its rock outcropping and soft sand, the beach was the prettiest he had ever seen.

But sometimes Ben had trouble with the visitors. Some were rude to him when he pointed out the beach rules. They sneered when he explained the rules were for their own safety. Most swimmers had never heard of rip currents. A few summers ago a man had almost drowned trying to save his niece caught in one of the currents.

The town had posted signs warning about the hazard. This year, at the start of the summer season, the local newspaper even ran a big story describing rip currents. The paper had printed pictures and diagrams. Ben had cut out all of them and mounted them on cardboard covered with plastic. He tacked the display to his lifeguard station. Whenever people took the time to look at it, they were always surprised and had a lot of questions.

"It's true," Ben would tell them. "Not even Olympic swimmers can beat some of these currents. They can whip along at eight feet per second. That's fast. And sometimes, they go hundreds of yards out into the ocean. That hasn't happened here, but we have had them one hundred yards long. You can't fool around with them."

Ben knew. He had been lucky to have a second chance. He had almost drowned in that rip current eight years ago. He wished others could understand the danger as clearly as he did. Whenever anyone was willing to listen, Ben told them all he knew about rip currents—including how scary it can be to get stuck in one.

"Many beaches have rip currents," he told people. "They often form around breaks in sandbars or at low points."

Wayside Beach had a number of these spots, he explained. When waves rolling in from deep water pile up along the shore, that extra water has to go somewhere. It collects and rushes out through the break in the sandbar, streaming like a river out to sea. Rip currents can be as narrow as fifty feet. But some of them can be fifty yards wide. On windy days, when the waves are bigger and moving faster, the danger from rip currents is greatest.

11

"Can you see them?" one boy asked Ben.

"Look over there," said Ben, pointing to a section of the beach where the sea was choppy. "That's one. Churning water is a sign of a rip current. See the line of seaweed moving out toward the ocean? That's another sign. The water in a rip current can be a different color from the water around it too."

Ben didn't want to scare people out of the ocean. He loved it too much for that. He just wanted them to be smart about it. Staying calm was important. He tried to emphasize that point the most.

"If you're ever caught in a rip current, don't fight it," he would say. "You probably won't win. But there are two things you can do. You can let it carry you out. Eventually the current will slow down. Then you can swim away from it and back to the beach. Or you can try swimming parallel to the beach right away. That way, you will slowly cut across the current and out of it. Either way, don't panic."

But most people who visited Wayside never got the talk on rip currents. They came to the beach to have fun, not to worry. Worrying was the lifeguard's job.

This summer, Ben seemed to be giving a lot of talks about rip currents. It was a hot summer, and the beach was very crowded. How could he watch so many people all at once?

To top it off, the wind hadn't stopped blowing. The surf was rough. Just about every day, the weather service warned of high risks for rip currents. Ben posted those warnings at his station. The wind and waves together could make the water dangerous for everyone, no matter how well they swam.

Sitting high on his lifeguard's chair, Ben spent each day tense and alert. He rarely took his eyes off the ocean. He scanned constantly for swimmers who might be in trouble. By the end of the day, he was worn out. His eyes ached from staring at the water. He was always glad when it was time to head home.

At six o'clock, all the lifeguards at Wayside went off duty. After that, people were supposed to stay out of the water. Signs posted along the beach made that clear.

One day, as Ben was rolling up his towel and getting ready to leave, a man stomped up to the lifeguard chair. He looked angry. A boy, about eleven, trailed behind him. The boy reminded Ben of himself when he was that age.

"I'm David Pew and I want an answer," said the man in a demanding voice. "Is it customary to close the beach this early?" He was standing with his hands on his hips. His legs were planted firmly in the sand. He stared arrogantly up at Ben. He looked as though he wanted to pick a fight.

"Uh oh," said Ben to himself. "This guy's going to be trouble." He made sure to answer in as pleasant a tone as he could.

"The beach isn't closed, sir," said Ben. "You can stay until the sun goes down. We just ask people not to swim. It's not safe without lifeguards."

"That's ridiculous," said Mr. Pew with a snort. "We've come a long way. We want to swim."

"I'm sorry, sir, but it's too dangerous with the rip currents," Ben explained.

"Never heard of them," said Mr. Pew, eyeing Ben with a mean, challenging look. "The water looks fine to me. There's a little surf, a nice breeze."

"I'm sorry, sir," said Ben again. "But those are the beach rules." Grabbing his towel, he jumped down from the chair. He turned to go and found himself standing face to face with Mr. Pew. He was glaring at Ben.

Ben could tell that Mr. Pew was a strong man. Judging by the size of his shoulders, he was probably a good swimmer too. The boy, on the other hand, looked light enough to be carried off on the tide like a piece of driftwood. Of course, Ben had been as scrawny once, and even then he could handle most kinds of rough water. Maybe this boy was the same.

"Enjoy the beach," said Ben as he stepped out of Mr. Pew's way. There was nothing else he could say.

Ben trudged across the sand and over to the far side of the parking lot where he had left his car in the shade of some tall trees. This was the best time of day at Wayside. The early evening light was soft. The air was cool. The beach was almost empty. Ben liked to turn the radio on in his car and relax for a while before driving home. He could enjoy the beach more when he didn't have to be responsible for the lives of everyone on it.

When he was a boy, had the lifeguards worried about him as much as he worried about the swimmers now? He realized now, as he sat in his car, that he must have made them nervous with the games he played. He probably looked as though he was drowning the way he pretended to be a jellyfish, floating limp and facedown in the water. Swimming so far out, as he liked to do, couldn't have made the lifeguards happy.

What if he had to watch a beach full of boys like himself? It would be much worse than having to deal with bullies, like Mr. Pew. Mr. Pew, and people like him, didn't cause any real trouble. They just made Ben angry. He could deal with that.

But people in danger was another matter. That's what set Ben on edge, and rip currents were definitely in that category.

Ben sat in his car with these thoughts. He was just about to leave when he saw someone running across the parking lot toward him. It was the boy who had been with Mr. Pew. He stuck his head through the window on the driver's side. His eyes were wide with fear.

"My dad's in trouble," said the boy. "He can't get back. The water's carrying him out. I told him you said it was too dangerous!"

Ben didn't wait to hear the rest of the story. He just hoped it wasn't too late to get to Mr. Pew.

Why had he gone swimming? Was he a show-off? Didn't he think the rules applied to him? Ben's mind raced with these questions as he tore across the parking lot to the shed where the lifeguards kept their rescue equipment.

"Three, fourteen, eleven . . ." Ben said, spinning the dial on the shed's combination lock. He prayed he would be able to yank it open quickly and get into the shed. Lately the lock hadn't worked well. Now it was still sticking.

Ben tried the combination again. No luck. A feeling of panic gripped him—the same freezing panic he had felt years ago when he was caught in the rip current.

"Stay calm," Ben told himself, remembering his lifeguard training classes. He grabbed the metal latch on the door of the shed and jerked it as hard as he could. The latch, the lock, and all the screws tumbled out of the rotten wood and the door swung open. Ben grabbed the first rescue tube he could find, slung it over his shoulder, and raced down to the beach.

The boy was there shouting at Mr. Pew to hold on. Ben plunged in, waded out a short distance, and almost immediately felt the tug of the current. It carried him quickly from the shore. By the time Ben reached Mr. Pew, he was struggling to keep his face above the water. A few seconds more and he would have gone under. Ben grabbed Mr. Pew and lifted his shoulders onto the tube. Mr. Pew's head rolled back and his eyes locked with Ben's for a moment. Fear had replaced the arrogant stare.

Suddenly Ben felt a rush of sympathy for this foolish man. He had gotten himself into a situation that he couldn't handle. Ben could still feel his own fear whenever he thought about how helpless he had felt in the rip current. It was a horrible feeling.

"Don't panic," Ben said in a firm, confident voice. "I'll get you back to shore." Slowly, with his arms wrapped around Mr. Pew and the rescue tube, Ben began to kick into the current. He inched across it, traveling parallel to the beach. It was only about ten yards to the edge of the current, but without Ben, Mr. Pew never would have made it. When they pushed through into still water, Ben felt a surge of relief.

"We're almost there," said Ben, kicking and breathing hard. When he finally dragged Mr. Pew onto the shore, the sun was going down. Ben sank down into the sand next to Mr. Pew. He was exhausted. Mr. Pew's son squatted on the other side.

Slowly Mr. Pew raised himself to his elbows. He stared hard at Ben for a moment.

"You saved my life," he said. "Thank you." Then he turned to the boy.

"And thank you for listening to him," he said to his son. "His good advice saved your life too."

Rip Currents

Playing in the surf on a beach can be a lot of fun. It can also be dangerous. More than eighty percent of the rescues on beaches with surf are because of rip currents. These currents are channels of water that rush from the shore out to sea. Rip currents also occur on the Great Lakes.

People call these currents by other names, such as rip tides and undertows. However, they are not tides and they don't tow swimmers under the water. What rip currents can do is catch swimmers in a stream of swiftly moving water and carry them away from the shore. Usually, rip currents flow between one and two feet per second. Sometimes they flow a lot faster. The danger comes when swimmers panic and try to fight against the current. They can become exhausted. That's when a drowning can happen.

What can you do to stay safe? Never swim alone. It's best to swim on beaches that have lifeguards. If you do get caught in a rip current, stay calm. Don't fight against it. The current will eventually end, and you will be able to swim back to shore. Tread water while the current carries you or swim parallel to the beach. You'll be able to get to the edge of the current and swim through calmer water.